1. This book may be kept three weeks. It is to be returned on / before the last date stamped below.
2. A fine of 25c will be charged for every week or part of week a book is overdue.

Hermes Tricks the Gods

Two Loves of Apollo

Halcyon Days

For Joe Jones

ORCHARD BOOKS
96 Leonard Street, London EC2A 4XD
Orchard Books Australia
Unit 31/56 O'Riordan Street, Alexandria, NSW 2015
This text was first published in Great Britain in the form of
a gift collection called *The Orchard Book of Greek Gods and Goddesses*,
illustrated by Emma Chichester Clark in 1997
This edition first published in hardback in Great Britain in 2000
First paperback publication 2001
Text © Geraldine McCaughrean 1997
Illustrations © Tony Ross 2000
The rights of Geraldine McCaughrean to be identified as the author and
Tony Ross as the illustrator of this work have been asserted by them in
accordance with the Copyright, Designs, and Patents Act, 1988
ISBN 1 84121 897 9 (hardback)
ISBN 1 84121 660 7 (paperback)
1 3 5 7 9 10 8 6 4 2 (hardback)
1 3 5 7 9 10 8 6 4 2 (paperback)
A CIP catalogue record for this book is available
from the British Library
Printed in Great Britain

HERMES TRICKS THE GODS

TWO LOVES OF APOLLO

HALCYON DAYS

GERALDINE MCCAUGHREAN

ILLUSTRATED BY TONY ROSS

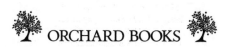

ORCHARD BOOKS

HERMES TRICKS THE GODS

The gods never grow old. Take Hermes. He is seventeen for all eternity, and the other gods never let him forget it. "Fetch this, Hermes. Do that, Hermes. Carry this message. Do as your half-brother tells you." He even cooks for them.

5

But Hermes doesn't mind. He's an easygoing boy. People down on Earth ask his protection when they go on journeys: some of those wild country roads swarm with thieves and ruffians. Mind you, the thieves and ruffians ask the help of Hermes, too. They've probably heard the stories of Hermes's childhood and how light-fingered he was, even as a baby!

The day Hermes was born – in a cave in Arcadia – his mother, Maia, laid him in his cradle and kissed his tufty hair. "Don't cry now. You are a son of Zeus and a secret from his wife. If she hears you are here, Hera will hate you with a deadly hatred, and kill you if she can. So hush, my little Hermes. Don't cry." In rocking the cradle, Maia herself went to sleep.

Hermes was a
big baby: big in the
morning and much
bigger by noon, when
he clambered out of
his cradle, toddled out of

the cave, and met a tortoise.
Banging on the
tortoise's shell, he
heard a throbbing
hollow noise he
liked. So, emptying
out the tortoise, he
tied threads of his

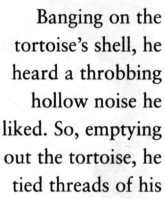

mother's hair round the shell.

When Maia stirred at
the pulling of her hair,
Hermes plucked a
tune which soothed
her back to sleep.

Then, slinging his newly invented lyre across his back, Hermes toddled away down the road, making up songs as he went. He was hungry. He wanted a drink of milk.

"Watch me go along,
To see what I can find.
Hear me sing my song,
With my lyre tied on behind.
I'm going to find a moo-cow
Maybe one or two cows:
I may just follow
My brother Apollo
And round up quite a few cows!"

All the way to Pieria he walked, growing all the while, and in the middle of the afternoon found the grazing place of Apollo's shining brown cows. They were all bursting with milk, and Hermes drank all he could drink.

Then, hazel switch in hand, he began to drive the cows back the way he had come. He did not drive them headfirst, but blipped their noses, and made them walk backwards, so that the tracks they left would look as if they had been coming, when rightly they had been going. He tied twigs to his little feet, as well, to scuff out his own footprints.

Back along the road he toddled, singing as he went, and picking grapes off the vines at the roadside. An old woman tending the vines straightened her aching back to watch him go by. It was a remarkable sight, after all: a baby toddling along in wicker shoes, driving a herd of back-to-front cows.

Hermes put a chubby finger to his lips, as if to say, "Don't breathe a word."

By the time he had hidden the cows –

up trees,

down holes,

under bushes –

Maia his mother was awake and standing at the door of the cave. "And where do you think you've been till this time of night?" she demanded, hands on hips.

Hermes climbed into his cradle: it was a bit small for him now – he had grown so much since morning.

"Never you mind, Mummy," he said. Then sucking his thumb, he quickly fell asleep.

When he woke,
Apollo was standing
over him, shouting
till the cave echoed.
"Where are my cows?"

"Agoo," said Hermes.

"You don't fool me. Where are my
cows, you thieving infant!"

"A-moo?" said Hermes, and chortled.

Apollo's golden hair
curled a little
tighter. "An old
woman saw a
baby driving my
cows this way.
Now get out
of bed. I'm
taking you before

the court of the gods! You can answer to
Almighty Zeus for your cattle-rustling!"

* * *

"Silence in court!" bellowed Zeus, as Hermes plucked his tortoise-lyre.

"Answer the charge! Is it true, Hermes, that you stole the cattle of Apollo?"

Hermes stood up. "Almighty gods... gentlemen... ladies... I appeal to you – do I look like a thief? Does it seem to you probable, does it seem to you likely, that I, a little child, a mewling infant, a child of rosy innocence, should walk fifty miles on the day of my birth and carry off – like some vagabond, some deceitful rapscallion – a herd of shining cows?"

"*Yes!*" bawled Apollo.

"Silence in court!"

"And me a vegetarian! A lover of animals! The merest silken butterfly fluttering over my crib is enough to make me laugh aloud at the wondrous beauty of Nature!"

"*Shyster!*" shouted Apollo.

"Silence in court!"

Hermes toddled about the courtroom, declaring his innocence, presenting his defence. He laid his baby curls on the knees of the goddesses and looked

earnestly into the eyes of the gods. He even hugged Apollo's knees, saying, "Would I steal from my own dear brother – child of my own beloved father, the mighty, the ineffable Zeus?"

Hera stood up with a scream of rage. "*Another* son of yours, Zeus?" She pointed a fearsome finger at Hermes. "For that I'll make you sorry you were ever born, baby!" then she slammed out of the courtroom.

"You were *seen*. There are *witnesses*," snarled Apollo at his little half-brother.

Hermes did not even blush, he simply took out his tortoise-lyre and began to play. Apollo stared at the extraordinary instrument, overwhelmed with envy.

"I never said I didn't *take* the cows," said Hermes. "I only said I didn't *steal* the cows. The truth is, I merely *borrowed* the cows. For a drink, you know. We babies, we need our milk if we're to grow into bigstrong boys. You ladies understand that, surely? Naturally, brother, you can have your cows back whenever you like. And as a token of goodwill, I'd like you to accept this lyre – I invented it yesterday."

The court cheered and clapped. Apollo snatched the lyre and began to pluck at it suspiciously. Zeus got to his feet.

"Hermes, son of Maia, you are plainly a rascal and a rogue. But you have clever fingers and a golden tongue. From this day forward, you shall be messenger of the gods...as soon as you have given back Apollo's shining cattle."

"Thank you, Daddy!" exclaimed Hermes. "Perhaps he might like these back too." From behind his back, Big Baby Hermes produced the bow and arrow he had stolen from Apollo when he hugged him. The jury of gods gasped and stamped their feet, laughing at the outrageous audacity of the child.

Even Apollo could not stay angry with a half-brother who had given him the first lyre in the world. They left court together, discussing philosophy and music, poetry and politics.

"You had better watch out for Queen Hera," Apollo warned his little half brother. "She hates you with a deadly hatred. She will never let you be messenger of the gods, no matter what Zeus says."

"Oh no? Would you like to bet on that?" replied Hermes. "If Hera drives me off Olympus, I shall teach you how to play that lyre of mine. If I make her like me, you can give me... what?... your magic wand. Agreed?"

"Agreed!" cried Apollo. "You haven't a chance."

"Well, please excuse me now," said Baby Hermes politely, "but it's time for my morning nap." He trotted away across the marble floors of Olympus, towards the hall of the Queen of Heaven.

He went to the cradle at the foot of her bed, and smiled down at her own baby son, Ares.

"Could I ask you a very great favour?" he said.

When Hera returned
to her room, she
lifted her baby,
swaddled in
lambswool, and
cradled him in
her arms. She
fed him, she sang
to him, she rocked
him – "My, what a
fine, big boy you
are!" – and plucking
back the swaddling from
round his head, she kissed his tufty hair.

"Agoo," said Hermes. "Guess who."

It was a risk. She has a nasty temper,
the Queen of Heaven. She might have
beaten his brains out then and there.
But she didn't. They say a woman can't
feed a baby and hate it afterwards.

Hera and Hermes get along well now, so long as he makes himself useful: cooking, running errands. So he won his bet with Apollo – won the magic wand, too, though he still gave Apollo music lessons. In exchange, Apollo taught his half-brother how to foretell the future.

Two Loves of Apollo

A god who thinks the world of himself must, of course, live at the centre of the world. No matter that the spot is guarded by a dragonish snake. Apollo simply wrestled the snake to a standstill, rattled it till its brains coddled, coiled it up like a rope, and set it on a tripod.

"From today you are my oracle," he said, staring into the snake's bloodshot eyes. "Let the magic of this place rise through the legs of this, your three-legged throne, and speak through you of Times to Come. The whole world will come here to question you. That means the whole world will come to the Temple of Apollo, here at the world's centre!"

And they did, of course. Because if there is one thing that you humans crave, above food and drink and wealth and love, it is to know what Fate holds in store for you.

Kings and heroes come from every corner of the Mediterranean to ask the Oracle, "Will I win this war?" "Who shall I marry?" "What must I fear?" "How shall I die?"

The answers screamed out by the Oracle, in her frenzied, banshee wail, may sound senseless, but somehow the visitors always make sense of them. They make their tributes to Apollo, the god of prophecy, and some whisper that Apollo is as great as Zeus – but not if Zeus is listening.

People come to Delphi for another reason too: for the Pythian Games, which Apollo holds there. Some whisper that the games are as splendid as those of his father, Zeus. But truly there was never anything to match the Olympian Games.

They draw the greatest sportsmen in the world – gods and demi-gods, heroes and princes. No slaves, no women, no foreigners are allowed within sight or sound of the field.

They run and jump

and throw the javelin
and the discus,

wrestle and compete as
though to lose was to die.

The only prize is fame and a wreath of green bay leaves – which the victor immediately tosses into a bonfire as a tribute of thanks to Zeus. And by the end of the games, that bonfire is a hill of pale-blue ash higher than any man could jump.

No one has won more laurel wreaths than Apollo. Still, he has been unlucky in other ways.

Apollo had a friend –
a little boy with lilac
eyes and fleecy hair,
called Hyacinthus. No
one in Greece would argue:
that boy was as beautiful as any
god – the most beautiful mortal ever born,
and with a nature to match. He only had to
enter a room and it was as if a torch had been
lit, a window opened on a warm night.
Everyone loved him. Everyone wanted to
have him to themselves – like a work of art
bid for at auction. Everyone wanted to own
Hyacinthus. But Apollo won him.

Hyacinthus thought the world of Apollo
who would take him riding in the sun's
chariot and teach him how to play music
and throw a discus. So Hyacinthus neglected
all his other friends – including Zephyrus,
the West Wind.

Zephyrus could not
bear to see Apollo
and the boy playing
and laughing together;
he howled in the
hollow trees and sea
caves, hissed with envy
through the treetops. Then he
swore that if he could not have
Hyacinthus, no one else would.

Apollo took Hyacinthus to the Olympic
Games; to show off to him,
as usual. His javelin
flew as far and
fast as a speeding
arrow, his discus
whirled like
a planet across
the sky. He was
magnificent.

Even those who pitted themselves against him had to admit it. The muscles flexed around his legs and shoulders like golden ropes binding a lion, and his mane of hair quivered in the sun. Hyacinthus was there in the crowd, standing up on his bench, shouting for his friend, half chanting, half singing: "Apollo is the victor of victors! A laurel crown for Apollo!"

Apollo smiled in his direction and waved. Then he bent his back, spread his arms and began to whirl about. That discus in his hand might have been the sun itself, he put such power into the throw.

But he did not see Zephyrus. No one did. There is no seeing Zephyrus. He is just a tree tossing, a breeze in the face, a

sudden sharp tug in the back of a cloak. As Apollo let fly the discus, Zephyrus blew. The breeze caught the bronze disc and carried it wildly off course. It would have carried much farther than any other – but instead it veered into the crowd and struck Hyacinthus just above the ear.

He was dead before he fell from the bench. Before he touched the ground, Apollo was there to catch him. But Hyacinthus was mortal. There was nothing Apollo could do about that.

"Oh, Zeus! Don't let his beauty be lost to the world for ever!" Apollo pleaded, distracted with misery.

And Zeus threw down a handful of
magic – like a farmer sowing seed.
Hyacinthus no longer lay
in Apollo's arms: he was
gone. Instead, a little
flower grew where
the boy's blood had
touched the grass.
It was the colour
of his eyes, and
on a warm night
through an
open window,
its scent steals
in like an
unseen
visitor.

No living soul can describe the sound of Apollo's sorrow that day. But Hyacinthus can. Inscribed in a deeper purple on every petal of the hyacinth are the very words of his grief, "Ai! Ai! Ai!"

HALCYON DAYS

Zephyrus, the West Wind, paid for his
unkindness (though no one guessed
his part in the killing).

Zephyrus had a daughter called
Halcyone – almost as lovely a girl as
Hyacinthus had been a boy. Like Apollo,
she too cared more for a mortal than
for all the gods put together. She married
him, too: a young sailor called Ceyx.

As Apollo wept, Zephyrus danced in a frenzy of triumph and wretchedness. For in his jealousy he had robbed Apollo but destroyed his own dear little friend. As he danced, he inadvertently whipped the sea into a summer storm, and crests of foam sank a dozen ships.

Ceyx was on board one of these ships.

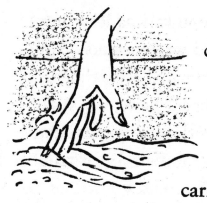

Zephyrus tried to comfort his daughter, but she would not be comforted. She sailed the sea in any vessel that would carry her – fishing boat, caïque or merchantman – leaning over the rail, sweeping the sea with her fingers, searching, searching, on and on, for her drowned husband. Angrily she brushed the blinding tears from her eyes, hoping to catch sight of his purple cloak, his green shirt. She called his name so loudly and unceasingly that her father could not make her hear any of his comforting words.

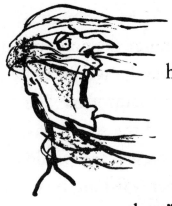

So the West Wind went to Olympus, and begged his fellow gods on bended knee: "Bring Ceyx back to life, or my daughter will die of grief!"

"You know I cannot do that," said Zeus. "Mortal man has only one short life, and then his soul belongs to Hades. That is the Law."

"I would spare his soul," said Hades, moved by the West Wind's tears. "See where it flies over the sea, towards the entrance to the Underworld? But his body is gone, so how shall he live again? It is impossible."

"Then let me die too!"

It was Halcyone, standing at the gate of Heaven. Across her arms hung a sodden cloak of purple and in her hands were scraps a of green shirt.

"Do you wish so much to be with this mortal that you would give up your immortality, child?" said Zeus.

"What is everlasting life to me, but everlasting sadness?" Halcyone replied. "Let me die!"

But Zeus did not grant her wish. Instead, he threw magic, like two handfuls of feathers, which settled gently over Halcyone and over the soul of Ceyx.

The next moment, two kingfishers darted out of the windows of Heaven – green and purple and a thousand other turquoise colours stolen from the sea.

They brushed wing-tips, they somersaulted and soared through the thin air and down towards the rivers and the sea. Halcyone and Ceyx were together again, and their love made them faster on the wing than any other bird – as though even eternity was too short a time to be together.

Once a year, Halcyone builds a nest of fishbones – a nest which floats on the sea – and there she lays her eggs. For fourteen days she sits brooding on her eggs, and while she does, her father tiptoes through the world with his finger to his lips, holding back every breath of wind for fear the floating nest should be disturbed.

They are his grandchildren, after all, those hatching bundles of beak and claw and feather. Every year he does it – sailors call that fortnight of dead calm the Halcyon Days – and the result is a world full of kingfishers. There goes one now!